For Franky and Sammy Kohn.

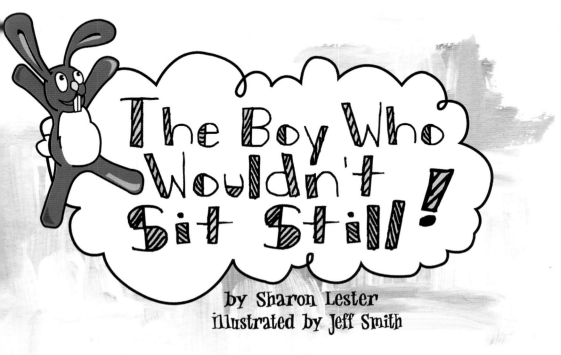

The Boy Who Wouldn't Sit Still!

by Sharon Lester

illustrated by Jeff Smith

PRIVILEGED COMMUNICATIONS, LLC

© 2008 by Sharon Lester
Printed in the U.S.A.
ISBN-13: 978-0-9802302-0-8
ISBN-10: 0-9802302-0-9

theboywhowouldntsitstill.com

There is a little boy who we all know

who has things to do
and places to go.

"He just won't sit still,"
is what you might say.

But let me explain a few things
and you'll understand it his way.

It starts the moment he wakes up in bed.
He has so many thoughts and ideas in his head!

It's hard for him
to lie still and rest.
What people don't realize is,
it's the things they suggest.

Ring

Ring

Ring

Ring

The first thing Mom says is,
"Go jump in the shower!"
Doesn't that mean
jump around for an hour?

He pretends he's on
a trampoline
splashing around
until he is clean!

Then at lunch
when Dad says,
"Can you please pass the bread?"

The boy does pass it –
right over his head!

He imagines himself
a football star.
He didn't know
the bread would travel so far!

“Time-out for you!” says Dad.
“Put your chair toward the wall!”

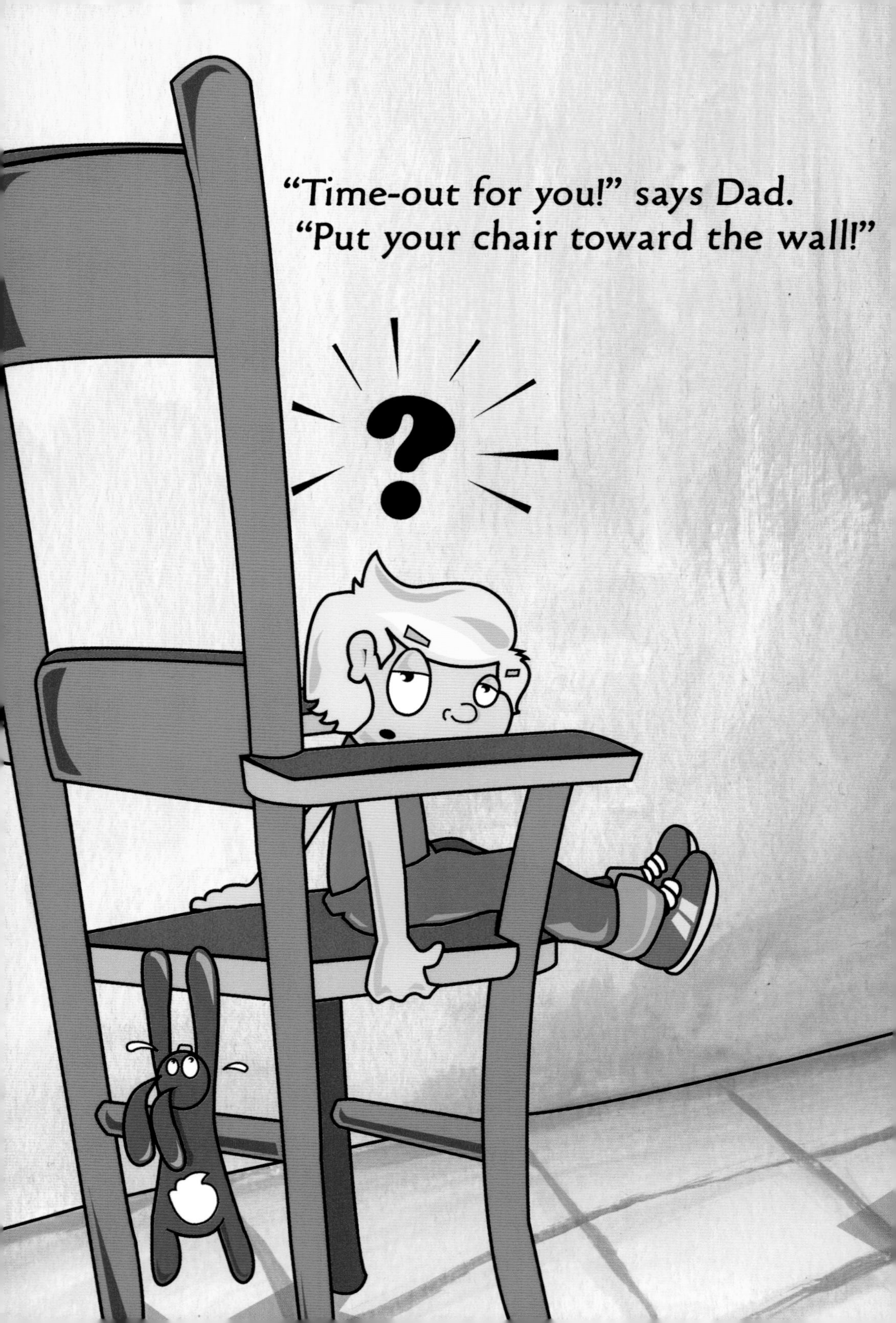

As the boy sits there
he feels very small.
He didn't want to get
in trouble at all!
He wonders why
what he hears people say
can make his thoughts
go a different way.

Then big sister tells him,
"Go pick up your room."

His mind starts to turn
and he thinks, "hmmm..."

So he stacks his toys on a chair
and the chair on the bed.
Then he lifts everything
right over his head!

It balances briefly
then crashes to the floor
just as big sister
appears at the door.

She looks kind of mad
as one would assume
but he was just trying
to pick up his room!

Then Grandma says,
"Go climb in the car."
He can certainly do that –
he's the best climber by far!

In through the window,
head down and knees bent.
His Grandma says firmly,
"That's not what I meant."

So you can imagine
when someone says,
"Let's run to the store,"

how his feet hit the ground
and he sprints for the door!

Or at night when Mom says,
"Can you hop into bed?"
Of course he can do
just what she said!

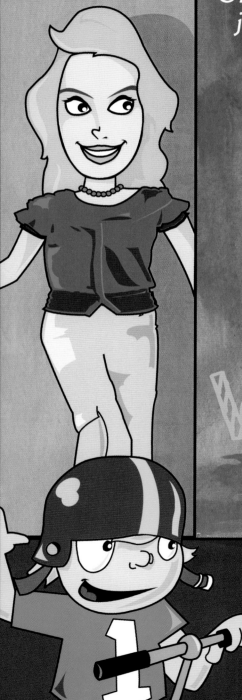

So he hops and he hops
and he hops all the way
and lays in bed thinking
of all he did that day.

He jumped in the shower
and passed the bread.

He picked his room up
right over his head!

He climbed in the car
and ran to the store.

He hopped into bed and
he could have done more!

Perhaps now you know
about things people say,
that words can be taken
in more than one way.

And that little boy
with so much still to do?
Maybe that little boy -

IS YOU!!!